—— THE INSIDER'S GUIDE TO ——

BOOSTING YOUR

SALESFORCE

BUSINESS

UNCOVERING THE SECRETS BEHIND STAGNANT GROWTH

—— THE INSIDER'S GUIDE TO ——

BOOSTING YOUR
SALESFORCE
BUSINESS

UNCOVERING THE SECRETS BEHIND STAGNANT GROWTH

POOJA SINGHAL

Worldwide Published by
Pendown Press

PENDOWN PRESS LLP

An ISO 9001 & ISO 14001 Certified Co.,

Regd. Office: 3767A, Kanhaiya Nagar,

Tri Nagar, Delhi-110035

Ph.: 8130886000, 9650072927, 8595249536

E-mail: info@pendownpress.com

Branch Office: 1A/2A, 20, Hari Sadan, Ansari Road,

Daryaganj, New Delhi-110002

Ph.: 011-45794768

Website: PendownPress.com

First Edition: 2023

Price: ₹209/-

ISBN: 978-93-5554-909-9

Layout and Cover Designed by Pendown Graphics Team

Printed and Bound in India by Thomson Press India Ltd.

CONTENTS

PREFACE

As the Managing Director at 360 DEGREE CLOUD, I have seen firsthand the importance of a successful Salesforce partnership in today's ever-changing IT services landscape. Whether you're a Salesforce practice owner, Salesforce CRM practice Head, sales or marketing professional, or just anyone interested in learning more about the Salesforce ecosystem, you too can appreciate the importance of running and growing a Salesforce practice successfully.

However, achieving sustainable growth can be challenging. Despite the immense potential, many partners struggle to unlock the full potential of their Salesforce business.

That's why I wrote The Insider's Guide to Boosting Your Salesforce Business: Uncovering the Secret Reasons for Stagnant Growth. Through this book, I offer you an insider's perspective on the challenges and opportunities that Salesforce partners face.

With over 14 years of extensive experience as a Business Strategist, I understand the importance of developing effective strategies for long-term success.

As an entrepreneur and an experienced Business Professional with a laser focus on company growth, I have overseen employee engagement and company culture, and key people operations at 360 DEGREE CLOUD.

Based on my extensive experience working with Salesforce partners across the globe, I provide actionable insights and best practices to help you navigate the complex Salesforce ecosystem and develop effective strategies for long-term success. My goal is to empower you with the knowledge and tools needed to overcome obstacles and achieve sustainable growth in your Salesforce business.

PRELUDE: ANDREW, THE SALESFORCE PRACTICE OWNER - A FAMILIAR STORY

Andrew had been working as a Salesforce SI Partner for many years. He had successfully implemented Sales Cloud and Service Cloud for his clients, and his business was doing well. However, he had set his sights on becoming the number one Salesforce Partner in his area and was determined to grow his business further.

But things were not as easy as they seemed. The industry was evolving rapidly, and Salesforce was introducing new products and features at an unprecedented pace. Customers were demanding more from their Salesforce partners, and the competition intensified.

Andrew realized he needed to upskill by attending webinars, workshops, and training sessions to learn about the latest Salesforce products and technologies.

However, he soon realized implementing Customer 360 was much more complex than the Sales Cloud and Service Cloud. He struggled to find the right expertise to help him with the implementation. This led to him losing some of his deals to competitors who better understood the new products and features.

The situation was not helped by the fact that enterprise businesses always went with multiple Salesforce clouds and required proven experience in implementing them. Andrew's lack of expertise in other Salesforce clouds meant he was losing out on enterprise-level projects.

As Salesforce continued to grow with its acquisitions of new products and the creation of industry-specific packages, Andrew found it increasingly difficult to keep up. Every customer was different, and their demands were different, making it hard for him to scale his practice.

Here are the key failures in Andrew's Salesforce SI Partner business:

- Lack of expertise in implementing Customer 360
- Losing deals to competitors who had a better understanding of the product
- Inability to offer a wider range of solutions and services, particularly in other Salesforce clouds
- Difficulty in winning enterprise-level projects due to the lack of proven experience in multiple Salesforce clouds

- Inability to keep up with the ever-changing nature of the Salesforce ecosystem and its latest trends and technologies.

Andrew's fate is only too familiar and touches a raw nerve for many Salesforce practice owners. The chapters ahead deal with mitigating these key failures head-on and avoiding a similar cycle of deterioration.

Chapter 1

INTRODUCTION: UNDERSTANDING THE SALESFORCE ECOSYSTEM AND ITS POTENTIAL

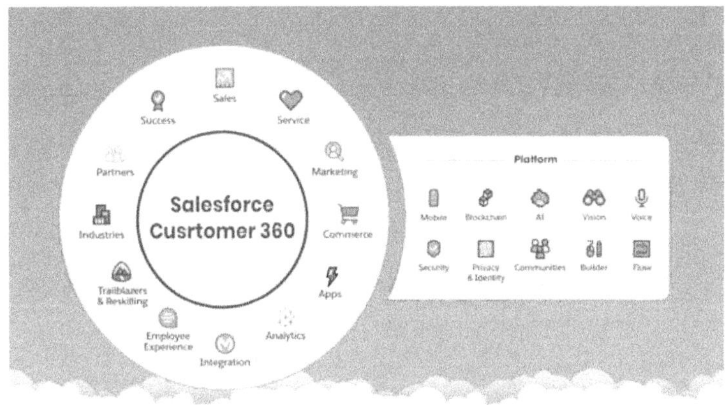

In this chapter, we will provide an overview of the Salesforce ecosystem and the opportunities it presents for partners looking to grow their businesses.

Salesforce is a leading provider of cloud-based software solutions that help businesses of all sizes manage their customer relationships, sales pipelines, marketing campaigns, and more. The Salesforce ecosystem is a vast network of partners, developers, and customers that leverage Salesforce's products and services to drive business growth and success.

The potential for growth within the Salesforce ecosystem is significant, with the company reporting strong revenue growth year over year. Partners in the ecosystem can tap into Salesforce's extensive customer base, leverage its suite of products and services, and benefit from its well-established brand recognition.

Additionally, Salesforce provides its partners with a comprehensive partner program that includes training, resources, and support to help partners build, market, and sell their solutions. By joining the Salesforce ecosystem, partners gain access to a powerful platform that can help them scale their businesses and achieve their growth objectives.

Throughout this book, we will explore the various strategies and tactics partners can use to unlock the full potential of their Salesforce partnerships and drive sustained growth. By understanding the Salesforce ecosystem and its opportunities, partners can develop a roadmap to success and thrive in this dynamic and exciting marketplace.

Chapter 2

EXAMINING THE CAUSES OF STAGNANT GROWTH IN SALESFORCE PARTNERSHIPS

In this chapter, we will take a deep dive into the various reasons why many partners are struggling to grow in the Salesforce ecosystem. While numerous factors can impact growth, some of the most common reasons for stagnation include the following:

1. **Lack of Clear Strategy**

   Many partners may not have a well-defined strategy in place to guide their growth. Without a clear roadmap, it can be challenging to identify the right target market, create effective messaging, and develop a plan to scale the business.

2. **Ineffective Sales and Marketing Strategies**

   Even with a clear strategy, partners may struggle to grow without executing effective sales and marketing campaigns. For example, partners may not effectively target the right audience or create compelling messaging to drive conversions.

3. **Failure to Differentiate**

   In an increasingly crowded marketplace, partners may struggle to stand out from competitors without effectively differentiating themselves. This can be especially challenging for partners offering similar services or solutions.

4. **Limited Resources**

   Some partners may be limited by their resources, making investing in growth initiatives difficult. For example, partners may not have the budget to hire additional staff or invest in technology.

5. Lack of Expertise

Partners may struggle to grow without the expertise or knowledge to effectively navigate the Salesforce ecosystem. This can include everything from technical knowledge to understanding the nuances of Salesforce's partner program.

By understanding these and other causes of stagnant growth in the Salesforce ecosystem, partners can begin to identify the root causes of their challenges and develop effective strategies to overcome them.

Chapter 3

THE IMPORTANCE OF EFFECTIVE SALES AND MARKETING STRATEGIES FOR SALESFORCE PARTNERSHIPS

In this chapter, we will explore the critical role that sales and marketing play in driving growth in the Salesforce ecosystem.

While there are numerous factors that can impact a partner's success, having effective sales and marketing strategies is essential for reaching new customers, building brand awareness, and driving revenue growth.

Effective Sales Strategies for Salesforce Partnerships

One of the most significant advantages of partnering with Salesforce is access to its extensive customer base.

However, partners must have a clear strategy in place to effectively identify and reach potential customers.

Here are some essential sales strategies for Salesforce partnerships:

1. Develop a Clear Value Proposition

Partners should develop a clear and compelling value proposition that highlights the unique benefits of their solution. This should be communicated in all sales materials and conversations to ensure potential customers understand the value of partnering with them.

2. Identify and Target the Right Audience

Partners should deeply understand their target audience and focus their sales efforts on reaching this group. This can be achieved through targeted marketing campaigns, personalized outreach, and other strategies.

3. Leverage Salesforce's Partner Program

Salesforce provides its partners with numerous resources and support to help them build, market, and sell their solutions. Partners should take full advantage of these programs to maximize their sales potential.

Effective Marketing Strategies for Salesforce Partnerships

In addition to effective sales strategies, partners must have a robust marketing strategy to drive brand awareness and attract new customers. Here are some essential marketing strategies for Salesforce partnerships:

1. Develop a Strong Brand

Partners should develop a strong brand identity that resonates with their target audience. This can be achieved through consistent messaging, branding, and design across all marketing materials.

2.   Utilize Content Marketing

Content marketing effectively attracts potential customers by providing valuable content that addresses their pain points and challenges. Partners can create blog posts, whitepapers, webinars, and other content highlighting their solutions' benefits.

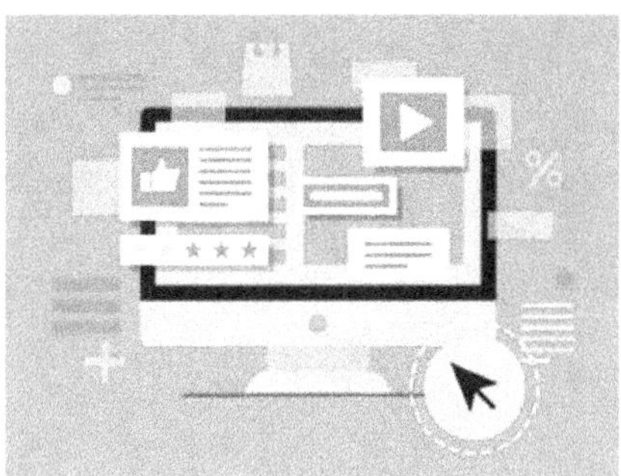

3.   Leverage Salesforce's Marketing Cloud

Salesforce provides its partners access to its Marketing Cloud, a powerful marketing automation platform. Partners should take full advantage of this tool to create targeted marketing campaigns that drive results.

Partners can drive sustained growth in the Salesforce ecosystem by developing effective sales and marketing strategies. Throughout the rest of this book, we will explore various tactics and best practices for achieving success in these critical areas.

Chapter 4

THE ROLE OF INNOVATION AND DIFFERENTIATION IN SALESFORCE PARTNER GROWTH

In this chapter, we will explore the critical role that innovation and differentiation play in driving growth for Salesforce partners. As the Salesforce ecosystem continues to evolve and expand, partners must find ways to differentiate themselves from the competition and innovate their solutions to meet customers' changing needs.

Importance of Innovation in Salesforce Partner Growth

Innovation is crucial for staying ahead of the competition in the Salesforce ecosystem. Customers are always looking for new and better solutions to their business challenges, and partners that can deliver innovative solutions are more likely to attract and retain customers.

Here are some ways that partners can drive innovation in their solutions:

1. Listen to Customer Feedback

Partners should actively listen to customer feedback to identify pain points and areas for improvement. This can help partners to develop innovative solutions that address these challenges.

2. Invest in Research and Development

Partners should invest in research and development to stay ahead of the curve and develop new and innovative solutions.

3. Explore Emerging Technologies

Partners should explore emerging technologies such as artificial intelligence, machine learning, and the Internet of Things to develop innovative solutions that can differentiate them from the competition.

The Importance of Differentiation in Salesforce Partner Growth

In addition to innovation, differentiation is essential for partners to stand out from the competition.

Differentiation can be achieved by developing unique solutions, offering exceptional customer service, or focusing on a specific niche within the Salesforce ecosystem.

Here are some ways that partners can differentiate themselves:

1. ## Develop Unique Solutions

    Partners should focus on developing unique solutions that provide clear benefits to their target audience. This can help them stand out in a crowded market and attract new customers.

2. ## Offer Exceptional Customer Service

    Partners should prioritize exceptional customer service to differentiate themselves from the competition. Partners can build long-term customer relationships and drive sustained growth by providing excellent support and service.

3. ## Focus on a Niche

    Partners can differentiate themselves by focusing on a specific niche within the Salesforce ecosystem. By specializing in a particular industry or solution, partners can become experts in their field and attract customers seeking specialized solutions.

By prioritizing innovation and differentiation, partners can stand out in the competitive Salesforce ecosystem and drive sustained business growth. Throughout the rest of this book, we will explore various strategies and tactics for achieving innovation and differentiation in the Salesforce ecosystem.

Chapter 5

THE IMPORTANCE OF BUILDING STRONG PARTNERSHIPS IN THE SALESFORCE ECOSYSTEM

In this chapter, we will explore the critical role that building strong partnerships plays in driving growth for Salesforce partners. In the Salesforce ecosystem, partners must work closely with other partners, customers, and Salesforce itself to achieve success.

Importance of Partnerships in Salesforce Partner Growth

Partnerships are essential for achieving growth in the Salesforce ecosystem. Here are some reasons why:

1. **Access to New Customers**

   Partnerships with other Salesforce partners can provide access to new customer bases and help partners to reach new markets.

2. Access to Expertise and Resources

Partnerships can provide access to expertise and resources that partners may not have, such as industry-specific knowledge or technical expertise.

3. Collaboration on Solutions

Partnerships can facilitate collaboration on developing innovative solutions that address complex customer challenges.

Building Strong Partnerships in the Salesforce Ecosystem

Building strong partnerships is essential for success in the Salesforce ecosystem. Here are some best practices for building strong partnerships:

1.   **Build Trust**

     Partnerships are built on trust. Partners should be transparent, honest, and reliable in their dealings with other partners, customers, as well as Salesforce.

2.   Communicate Effectively

Clear and open communication is essential for building strong partnerships. Partners should communicate regularly and effectively to ensure all parties are on the same page.

3.   Focus on Shared Goals

Partnerships should be built on shared goals and objectives. Partners should work together to develop a shared vision for success and collaborate on achieving these goals.

4.   Leverage Salesforce's Partner Program

Salesforce's partner program provides numerous resources and support to help partners build strong partnerships. Partners should take full advantage of these resources to drive sustained growth.

Conclusion

Building strong partnerships in the Salesforce ecosystem is essential for sustained growth. Partners can access new customers, expertise, and resources by prioritizing partnerships, collaborating on innovative solutions, and achieving shared goals. Throughout the rest of this book, we will explore various strategies and best practices for building strong partnerships in the Salesforce ecosystem.

Chapter 6

STRATEGIES FOR SCALING YOUR SALESFORCE PARTNER BUSINESS

In this chapter, we will explore various strategies for scaling your Salesforce partner business. As partners grow and mature in the Salesforce ecosystem, they must find ways to scale their operations, processes, and teams to meet the growing demand for their solutions.

Strategies for Scaling Your Salesforce Partner Business

1. ### Develop a Scalable Business Model

   Partners should develop a scalable business model that can grow and adapt to meet the changing needs of the market. This may involve investing in new technologies, processes, and people to streamline operations and increase efficiency.

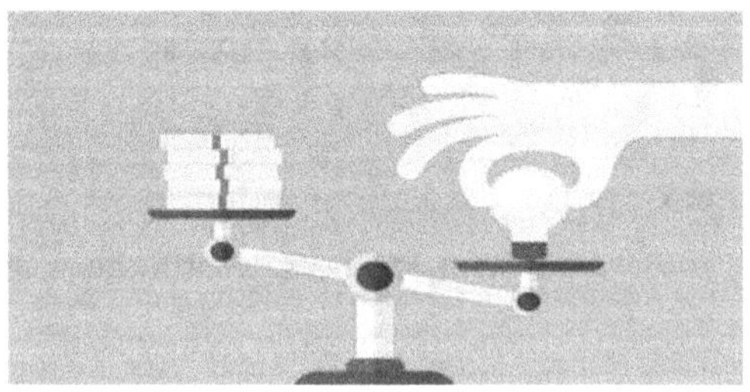

2. Expand Your Solution Offerings

Partners should look for opportunities to expand their solution offerings to meet the evolving needs of their customers. This may involve developing new products or services or expanding into new markets or industries.

3. Focus on Customer Success

Customer success is critical for driving sustained growth in the Salesforce ecosystem. Partners should prioritize customer success by delivering exceptional customer service, providing ongoing support and training, and continually improving their solutions to meet customer needs.

4. Build a Strong Team

As partners scale their operations, they must build a strong team to support their growth. This may involve hiring new employees, developing training programs, and creating a culture of collaboration and innovation.

5. Leverage Salesforce's Partner Program

Salesforce's partner program provides numerous resources and support to help partners scale their businesses. Partners should take full advantage of these resources, including training, marketing support, and access to Salesforce's extensive customer base.

Conclusion

Scaling a Salesforce partner business requires a combination of strategic planning, operational excellence, and a customer-centric approach.

By developing a scalable business model, expanding solution offerings, prioritizing customer success, building a strong team, and leveraging Salesforce's partner program, partners can achieve sustained growth and success in the Salesforce ecosystem.

Throughout the rest of this book, we will explore various strategies and best practices for scaling a Salesforce partner business.

Chapter 7

NAVIGATING CHALLENGES IN THE SALESFORCE ECOSYSTEM

In this chapter, we will explore the various challenges that partners may face in the Salesforce ecosystem and strategies for navigating these challenges.

Challenges in the Salesforce Ecosystem

1. Competition

The Salesforce ecosystem is highly competitive, with many partners vying for the same customers and opportunities. Partners must find ways to differentiate themselves from their competitors to succeed.

2.   Rapid Technological Change

The pace of technological change in the Salesforce ecosystem is rapid, and partners must stay ahead of the curve to remain relevant. This may involve investing in new technologies, processes, and people to stay competitive.

3.   Shifting Customer Needs

Customer needs and expectations are continually evolving, and partners must be able to adapt to these changes to remain successful. This may involve developing new solutions or customizing existing ones to meet customer needs.

4.   Limited Resources

Many partners in the Salesforce ecosystem are small and medium-sized businesses with limited resources. Partners must find ways to do more with less and prioritize their investments to achieve the greatest impact.

Strategies for Navigating Challenges in the Salesforce Ecosystem

1.   Differentiate Yourself

Partners must find ways to differentiate themselves from their competitors. This may involve developing unique solutions, offering exceptional customer service, or developing expertise in a particular industry or market.

2. Stay Ahead of the Curve

Partners must stay ahead of the curve by investing in new technologies, processes, and people to remain competitive. Partners should keep abreast of industry trends and attend industry events to stay informed.

3. Stay Close to Customers

Partners must stay close to their customers to continually understand their needs and expectations. This may involve conducting regular customer surveys, providing ongoing support and training, and developing strong relationships with key customers.

4.   Prioritize Investments

Partners must prioritize their investments to achieve the greatest impact. This may involve investing in areas that provide the most significant return on investment, such as customer success, marketing, or product development.

Conclusion

The Salesforce ecosystem presents both opportunities and challenges for partners. Partners can successfully navigate these challenges by differentiating themselves from their competitors, staying ahead of the curve, staying close to customers, and prioritizing investments. Throughout the rest of this book, we will explore various strategies and best practices for navigating challenges in the Salesforce ecosystem.

Chapter 8

LEVERAGING THE POWER OF PARTNERSHIPS IN THE SALESFORCE ECOSYSTEM

In this chapter, we will explore the power of partnerships in the Salesforce ecosystem and how partners can leverage these relationships to drive growth and success.

Partnerships in the Salesforce Ecosystem

The Salesforce ecosystem is built on a foundation of partnerships. Partnerships between Salesforce and its partners, between partners and customers, and between partners themselves are critical for driving growth and success in the ecosystem.

1. Partnership with Salesforce

Partnerships with Salesforce provide partners with access to resources and support that can help them grow and succeed. Salesforce offers a robust partner program that provides training, marketing support, and access to Salesforce's vast customer base.

2. Partnership with Customers

Partnerships are critical for customer success and long-term relationships. Partners should focus on delivering exceptional customer service, providing ongoing support and training, and continually improving their solutions to meet customer needs.

3. Partnership with Other Partners

Partnerships with other partners can be beneficial for driving growth and expanding solution offerings. Partners can collaborate on joint solutions or refer customers to each other to provide a broader range of services.

Strategies for Leveraging Partnerships in the Salesforce Ecosystem

1. Develop Strong Relationships

Developing strong relationships with Salesforce, customers, and other partners is critical for leveraging partnerships successfully. Partners should focus on building trust, communicating effectively, and collaborating on joint initiatives.

2. Create Joint Solutions

Partners can leverage partnerships to create joint solutions that meet customers' evolving needs. Partners should focus on developing solutions that complement each other's strengths and address customer pain points effectively.

3. Referral Programs

Partners can refer customers to other partners to provide a broader range of services. Referral programs can be an effective way to expand solution offerings and drive growth.

4.   Co-Marketing

Partners can collaborate on marketing initiatives to reach a broader audience and drive awareness of their solutions. Co-marketing initiatives can include joint webinars, social media campaigns, and events.

Conclusion

Partnerships are a critical component of the Salesforce ecosystem, and partners must leverage these relationships to drive growth and success. Partners can leverage partnerships successfully by developing strong relationships, creating joint solutions, implementing referral programs, and collaborating on co-marketing initiatives. Throughout the rest of this book, we will explore various strategies and best practices for leveraging partnerships in the Salesforce ecosystem.

Chapter 9

BEST PRACTICES FOR MARKETING AND SALES IN THE SALESFORCE ECOSYSTEM

Marketing Best Practices

1. **Develop a Clear Value Proposition**

   Partners should clearly communicate their unique value proposition to potential customers. This includes understanding customer pain points and how the partner's solution can address these pain points effectively.

2. **Leverage Digital Marketing**

   Digital marketing can effectively reach a broad audience and generate leads. Partners should create high-quality content, optimize their websites for search engines, and leverage social media channels to reach their target audience.

3.   Attend Industry Events

These events can effectively generate leads, network with other partners and customers, and stay current on industry trends.

Sales Best Practices

1.   Build Strong Relationships

Building strong relationships with potential customers is critical for closing deals. Partners should focus on developing trust, understanding customer needs, and providing exceptional customer service.

2.   Qualify Leads Effectively

Partners should focus on qualifying leads effectively to ensure they target the right customers with the right solution. This includes understanding the customer's pain points, budget, and decision-making process.

3.   Implement a Sales Process

A structured sales process can help partners close deals more effectively. This includes identifying key decision-makers, understanding the customer's needs and pain points, and presenting a tailored solution.

Conclusion

Marketing and sales are critical components of driving growth and success in the Salesforce ecosystem. By developing a clear value proposition, leveraging digital marketing, attending industry events, building strong relationships, qualifying leads effectively, and implementing a structured sales process, partners can effectively reach their target audience, generate leads, and close deals. Throughout the rest of this book, we will explore various marketing and sales strategies and best practices for success in the Salesforce ecosystem.

Chapter 10

DEVELOPING A CUSTOMER SUCCESS STRATEGY FOR LONG-TERM GROWTH

In this chapter, we will explore the importance of developing a customer success strategy for long-term growth in the Salesforce ecosystem. Customer success ensures that customers derive maximum value from a partner's solution and are satisfied with their experience. A strong customer success strategy can lead to increased customer retention, referrals, and long-term growth for the partner.

1. Understanding Customer Needs

The first step in developing a customer success strategy is to understand customer needs. This includes understanding their pain points, goals, and objectives. By understanding customer needs, partners can ensure that their solution effectively meets customer requirements.

2. Onboarding and Training

Onboarding and training are critical components of customer success. Partners should focus on providing effective onboarding and training to ensure that customers use the solution effectively and efficiently. This includes providing training on product features, best practices, and any customizations that have been made.

3. Ongoing Support and Engagement

Providing ongoing support and engagement is essential for ensuring customer success. Partners should focus on providing timely and effective customer support when issues arise. This includes having a strong support team in place, providing resources such as a knowledge base, and actively engaging with customers to ensure their needs are met.

4. Measuring and Tracking Success

Measuring and tracking customer success is critical for understanding how well a partner's solution meets customer needs. Partners should track key metrics such as customer satisfaction, product adoption, and retention rates. This information can be used to identify areas where improvements can be made and to develop strategies for continued growth.

Conclusion

Developing a customer success strategy is critical for long-term growth in the Salesforce ecosystem. By understanding customer needs, providing effective onboarding and training, providing ongoing support and engagement, and measuring and tracking success, partners can ensure that their solution effectively meets customer requirements and drives business growth.

EPILOGUE: ANDREW STRIKES BACK-
A NOT-SO-FAMILIAR COMEBACK
STORY

When Andrew got to know that he was not able to grow, he tried multiple ways and then failed again, but finally, he got the right advice to grow, and that has helped in growing his practice with more money and happiness.

He had worked hard to grow his company, but he found himself struggling to keep up with the pace of the ever-changing Salesforce ecosystem. Andrew followed the typical way to grow his company by hiring freelancers from different sources. Still, he was not the priority for these freelancers as they were working for multiple clients.

The same challenge occurred with the freelancers' expertise, and he had to look for a new freelancer for every skill set.

Andrew tried but failed once again because it was not feasible, and coordination was a big problem.

After the failure of the freelance hiring strategy, Andrew decided to hire an in-house team. However, hiring is not easy, and it is hard to find the right talent. After interviewing resources, Andrew had to wait for their contract period to end before joining him, and sometimes these resources still didn't join him.

That means, after being strung along for 3 months, he could still find out the candidate wasn't joining him at the last minute. This was very frustrating for him, and he eventually figured out that this wasn't scalable and he would not be able to grow the practice this way.

Andrew was looking now open to good advice, and one of his friends gave him the advice to work with a Salesforce Partner-one that has a big practice in Salesforce and has expertise in all Salesforce clouds. The idea here was that Andrew could then access all their resources for their skill sets and piggyback on their experience to onboard new customers and grow his practice.

Andrew started working with an offshore Salesforce Partner, and the most important benefit was that due to offshoring, it was very cost-effective. The partner was seasoned and practiced in each cloud, which helped him in the pre-sales, and after onboarding the customer, they could deliver the project.

Working with a Salesforce Summit Partner was finally the key to Andrew's success. The benefits of collaborating with a Salesforce Summit Partner are numerous: a broad range of expertise, including all the Salesforce clouds; a proven track record of success, which can help you build your brand and grow your business; and extensive experience in delivering complex projects, which can help you deliver your projects on time and within budget.

Working with a Salesforce Summit Partner can help you succeed by sharing access to the best Salesforce talent.

They have a team of certified Salesforce experts who can help you develop and execute your Salesforce strategy and provide the necessary support to help you grow your business, including marketing and sales support.

In conclusion, working with a Salesforce Summit Partner is the key to success in the Salesforce ecosystem. They can provide you with access to the best Salesforce talent, help you develop and execute your Salesforce strategy, and provide the necessary support to help you grow your business.

So, if you want to grow your business and achieve success in the Salesforce ecosystem, working with a Salesforce Summit Partner is the way to go.

We hope after Andrew's initial struggles in this book, his comeback as a cost-effective and delivery-focused Salesforce practice has given you some catharsis.

Here are some key takeaways on Andrew's success after collaborating with the Salesforce Summit Partner:

- Access to a wider range of skill sets and expertise in all Salesforce clouds

- Cost-effective offshoring of resources for development and support

- The ability to handle multiple projects at once without worrying about the availability of resources

- Improved coordination and collaboration between teams due to a shared understanding of the Salesforce platform

- Greater pre-sales support, including industry-specific solutions and packaged services

- Faster time-to-market for projects due to increased efficiency and expertise

- Better customer satisfaction, as Andrew was able to provide a comprehensive and integrated solution for customer 360 and other Salesforce requirements

- Increased revenue and profitability, as Andrew was able to expand his business by taking on larger enterprise customers with complex Salesforce needs

- A more stable and reliable workforce, as Andrew, was no longer reliant on external hires but had a dedicated team of experts working alongside him.

NEXT STEPS:
LET'S STAY IN TOUCH

Whew you've taken in so many insights. You need to take a minute and pat yourself on the back.

I can say, without a doubt, that you've come farther than most. You are now armed with the knowledge that most Salesforce Practice Owners wished some shared with them when they were starting.

I hope the insights and strategies presented in these pages will help you unlock the full potential of your Salesforce partnership. But that alone won't be enough.

NO SIR; nothing ventured, nothing gained. A quiet reading without implementation is the same as learning to swim from a manual.

Luckily, this book is self-contained and lists all the steps you need to take to finally grow your Salesforce Practice even more. It's a self-help book.

But from experience, I also know a lot of readers, and Salesforce Practice owners won't get around to implementing even these critical, transformative steps.

They're just too caught up in their current commitments, wearing multiple hats, and in the inertia of the way they've always done business. And those businesses, dare I say, are at the same junction when I meet them months later.

So the way I see it, you now have 2 choices:

A - Keep doing things the way you've done them, OR

B - Introduce an agent of change, a guiding hand.

If you'd like to finally change the way you operate, hold my hand, and I'll ensure that you implement the practices shared in this book over the next 2 months.

As a reader of this book, my doors are always open for you.

You went through this book because, at some level, you're ready to see a change in your organization. It means you're open to change and improvement and ready to accept help.

And that's who I look forward to helping the most and also the kind of Salesforce team I enjoy working with. I'm all set to be your partner and change agent and embark on a memorable journey of growth for your Salesforce practice.

That's why, as a reader of this book, I'd love to provide you with an hour-long one-on-one consultation free of cost.

You simply need to reach out to me at

pooja@360degreecloud.com.

Or connect with me on LinkedIn at

linkedin.com/in/pooja360degreecloud/.

You could also just scan the QR code to connect with me on LinkedIn. Let's work together to achieve sustainable growth in your Salesforce business!

NOTES:

NOTES:

NOTES:

NOTES:

NOTES: